AF271460

The Scandal of the Parables

Diana Culbertson, OP

The Center for Learning

About the Author

Diana Culbertson, OP, is a professor emerita at Kent State University, where she directed the program of Religious Studies and the graduate program in Liberal Studies. She earned her Ph.D. in Comparative Literature and holds M.A. degrees in English and Theology. She lectures and writes extensively and is the author of *The Meaning of Faith, The Meaning of Hope,* and *God in a World of Violence,* all Center for Learning publications.

The Publishing Team

Rose Schaffer, HM, M.A., President/Chief Executive Officer
Bernadette Vetter, HM, M.A., Vice President
Mary Jane Simmons, HM, M.A.,Vice President, Editorial
Linda Valasik, HM, M.M., Coordinator, Religion Division
Carla Fritsch, M.A., Editor
Tammy Sanderell, B.A., Editor

Nihil Obstat

The Reverend Thomas H. Weber, STL, SSL
Censor Deputatus

Imprimatur

The Most Reverend Anthony M. Pilla, D.D., M.A.
Bishop of Cleveland

Given at Cleveland, Ohio, on 2 December 2002.

The Nihil Obstat and Imprimatur are official declarations that a book or pamphlet is free of doctrinal or moral error. No implication is contained therein that those who have granted the Nihil Obstat and Imprimatur agree with the contents, opinions, or statements expressed.

ISBN-13: 978-1-56077-729-8
ISBN-10: 1-56077-729-X

Contents

Spirituality for Adult Christians is a faith formation series that brings theological insights to both the current life experiences of adults and particular subjects of interest that contribute to the development of adult spirituality. These insights can invite personal conversation and therefore lead to the transformation of society according to the values of the Gospel.

Spirituality is a person's relationship to God. The call to grow deeper in spirituality is often heard through the connection to a faith community and developed through formal and informal daily ministry. Real-life situations reveal the concrete and dynamic character of the relationship.

The series clearly mirrors the direction of the Second Vatican Council in this postconciliar time and captures the insights of the disciplines of psychology, sociology, history, and economics as well. Since spirituality is a characteristic of people of every religion, interfaith and ecumenical dialogue also contribute to an understanding of spiritual growth. This series is meant to be a support for adults who want to understand and live their developing relationship with God in more meaningful and committed ways. Although these books are directed to small faith-sharing groups, individuals seeking spiritual growth are also encouraged to use the series for personal reflection.

Prayer begins and concludes each session. Within the flexible one-and-a-half- to two-hour time frame are two periods of reflective input, each followed by a conversation time to process questions that focus on personal integration of the values of the Gospel. The session draws to a close with a time of silent reflection and/or journaling. Participants should bring a small notebook if they wish to journal. The opportunity to clarify one's thoughts, interiorly or with private writing, can facilitate faith sharing. This personal time is followed by a discussion of individual or communal action, an essential step, in order to live the conversion that true growth in faith requires. Resources for prayer during the session and for continued growth in the days ahead are listed at the end of each session. After prayer, time is spent socializing.

This series, *Spirituality for Adult Christians*, provides a structure for faith formation that joins together emerging lay leaders in the Body of Christ today, as family members, as Church, as participants in the global village.

How to Use This Book

Time	Session Outline	Notes
	Gathering Time	Reconnect while informally coming together.
2 min.	Overview	Begin together by having a leader or volunteers read these sections aloud.
2 min.	Focus	
3 min.	Opening Prayer	Center minds and hearts by using the given format, or praying aloud together, or asking for a volunteer to lead the group. Do the same for the Closing Prayer. Check your local religious bookstore for cassette tapes and CDs.
10 min.	Group Reflection I	Consider the Group Reflection together through silent reading, shared reading aloud, or by enlisting the leader as reader. Individual reading before the session is also an option.
15 min.	Conversation	
10 min.	Group Reflection II	
15 min.	Conversation	
		Use the Conversation portion to probe the implications of the topic for your life by listening to ideas and asking questions that shed light on your adult faith journey.
15 min.	Silent Reflection/ Journal Comments	Embrace silence and listen to the voice of the Holy Spirit within. Write about this experience if it clarifies God's call.
15 min.	Invitation to Conversion	Discuss this action step, or plan one that may be more meaningful. If possible, make a verbal commitment to the activity.
3 min.	Closing Prayer	
20 min.	Social Time	
	Resources for Prayer in This Session	Enrich this session with these elements.
	Resources for Continued Growth	Explore these references individually for broader understanding and continued reflection on the topic.

The Scandal of the Parables

Introduction

The spiritual writer Anthony Bloom once remarked that one of the reasons which prevent us from being truly ourselves and finding our own way is that we do not realize the extent to which we are blind. We may have had the experience of arguing with someone who was completely unaware of what he or she didn't know. Our conversation in those circumstances can break down completely. But the situation can be reversed. Stubborn insistence on the wrong idea is frequently disastrous, especially since we often believe that our own idea is so obvious, so clear that anyone who disagrees with it must surely be uninformed. We all must realize the extent to which we are blind. Without that awareness, we cannot learn anything.

The parables of Jesus were directed to good people with strong ideas. The difficulty of many of his listeners was that they didn't know the extent of their blindness. Describing the kingdom of God to those whose idea of salvation was liberation from the Romans; describing God to people whose ideas were formed from thousands of years of tradition and conflict; speaking of love and charity to listeners who were traditionally convinced that charity begins—and ends—at home required a way of teaching that was radically distinct from simple instruction.

The parables of Jesus, his life, and especially the manner of his death was revelatory, not merely instructive. To understand the parables, to see them anew with fresh eyes, we need to remind ourselves of the cultural circumstances in which they were told, the function of their curious little plots, and the obstacle to traditional thinking they so often posed. We need to hear them again, transposing them, if possible, into our own culture, and experiencing their shock value. We cannot tame Christianity, making it so familiar, so bland, that we forget its revelatory power, its demands. One way to reeducate ourselves to the power of the Gospel is to examine the power of the parables. In these brief narratives, we glimpse something of the kingdom of heaven—especially if we are willing to admit our blindness.

Understanding Religious Language

Gathering Time

Overview

Scholars have always known that God cannot be described objectively as if the Infinite, all-loving, eternal, creative Presence could be contained in language. Language can only *point* to reality. Language is a symbol or sign of what we are thinking about. St. Thomas Aquinas, who wrote volumes about God, commented once that we can only speak of what God is not. We can say that God is *not* finite, *not* mortal, *not* powerless, *not* unknowing. We can say that God *is*, that God *is* existence, and without God, nothing exists. Yet, despite our limitations, we continue to speak of God. We struggle to find in our own existence the traces of God, the signs of God's presence, the clues to God's life and love in and around us. For Christians, Jesus is the unsurpassable Word of God, the one who above all others and beyond all books reveals who God is for us and how God is present to us. To study the preaching of Jesus is to see how this Word of God used human words and human existence to describe the one he knew as no one else in history ever knew. "You do not know him," Jesus said to his opponents, "but I know him" (*John 8:55*). How, then, did Jesus speak of his Abba, his own Father?

Focus

This session will examine why language about God must be indirect and why the preaching of Jesus seemed so often to confuse his listeners. Even his disciples complained that he was always talking in parables (*Matthew 13:10*). Why didn't he speak more directly? What is the advantage of language that uses human experience to speak of divine realities?

Opening Prayer

Leader: Lord, open our hearts and minds by the power of your Holy Spirit. Grant us the grace to live in faith, to hear the Word with joy, and to treasure it in our hearts.

All: Your Word is a lamp to our feet and a light to our path.

Leader: God, Lord of mercy, with you is Wisdom who knows
    your works
    and was present when you made the world.
Send her forth from your holy heavens.

All: Your Word is a lamp to our feet and a light to our path.

Leader: Scarce do we guess the things on earth,
    and what is within our grasp we find with
      difficulty;
But when things are in heaven, who can search them
    out?
    Or who ever knew your counsel, except you
      had given Wisdom
    and sent your holy spirit from on high?
                    (*Wisdom 9:17*)

All: Open our hearts and minds by the power of your Spirit. Renew the face of the earth, and make glad the whole world. We ask this in the name of Jesus, your Son.
Amen.

Group Reflection I: Speaking of God in Metaphor

A metaphor uses words that link known experience to unknown reality. We often joke about "the birds, the bees, and the butterflies," but speaking to a child about unknown experience requires entering the child's world and using a child's capacity to imagine. We have trouble imagining things that we've never heard of. When we do hear of something beyond our experience, we may imagine it in bizarre and strange ways, like the early European view of America as peopled by bearded natives who lived in a golden paradise.

Because religious language testifies to what we have never experienced, metaphor is essential to its expression. "No one has ever seen God," writes the author of the Fourth Gospel, adding that "the only Son . . . has revealed him" (*1:18*). If no one has ever seen God, how do we imagine all that God is for us? How does Jesus help us to imagine God? How do we measure our human experience against what Jesus has told us about his Abba, his Father in heaven?

How did Jesus talk to us? What could he say about the one he knew so well and whom we consistently misunderstand? Jesus could only talk to us in terms of what we know. At the same time, he had to speak in such a way that our limited imaginings were not simply confirmed. Do we imagine pearly gates and golden streets? Jesus didn't mention them. Do we imagine a God who limits access to heaven to those who are righteous and who obey the law? Jesus didn't suggest this as a possibility. Do we imagine a God who is pleased by long prayers, conspicuous fasting, and public righteousness? Jesus didn't praise this kind of behavior.

Metaphoric language has as its purpose to lead us into completely new meaning, meaning that would otherwise be inaccessible. When metaphor is taken literally, it loses its meaning and seems absurd. "In my Father's house there are many dwelling places [sometimes translated as "mansions"]. . . . I am going to prepare a place for you" (*John 14:2*). We have to stretch to discover exactly what these words of Jesus mean—and stretching doesn't get us very far. On the literal level, these words make no sense. There probably aren't any houses in heaven. On the metaphoric level, we understand something about our relationship to the Risen Jesus that would otherwise be totally inaccessible. We are led into the mystery of our own resurrection. We are led beyond our capacity to think logically. We are led into the darkness of faith, but that is quite different from the darkness of ignorance.

Jesus used metaphoric language often, sometimes in brief aphorisms, such as "[G]uard against the leaven of the Pharisees and the leaven of Herod," a comment that initially confused the disciples, who had to ask him what he was talking about (*Mark 8:15*). Another time he commented, "[I]f your foot causes you to sin, cut it off" (*Mark 9:45*). That suggestion should probably not be taken literally, but its metaphoric meaning is very powerful.

Parables are metaphoric language. Most of them are not simple allegories. The kingdom of heaven is not like yeast at all, but Jesus spoke of it as a kind of yeast which a woman puts into dough. He was trying to make a point that would otherwise be inaccessible to his audience. They would perhaps have imagined the kingdom more like the throne room of an Oriental potentate or in terms of the expulsion of the Roman occupiers of Palestine. That conquest would be—in their terms—"the restoration of the kingdom." They must have been bewildered by the description of the kingdom in terms of a woman making bread. So metaphoric language can actually lead us into confusion. In that confusion, however, lies the impulse to move beyond our expectations into real hope, and beyond our preconceptions into the infinite mystery of God's love. Jesus tried to move us beyond all of our cultural and personal limitations into the vastness of God's universe. That is what parables are about and why they were often disturbing to his listeners, people like us who sometimes didn't want to be disturbed too much.

Conversation

1. *Describe an experience that revealed to you how your hopes and imagination were distorted.*

    How did you deal with your disappointment?

2. *Has any experience in your life turned out to be much better or wildly different from what you had expected? How do you account for this?*

3. *Has God ever surprised you? Explain.*

4. *Has religious instruction or study ever changed your ideas about God? very much? Explain.*

5. *Do you know anyone whose ideas about God seem distorted to you? What accounts for these distortions?*

Group Reflection II: Speaking of God in Story

The Gospel writers did not compose theological essays. They told a story, and within that story were other stories, accounts of Jesus' debates with religious authorities, descriptions of healings and the reactions of those who witnessed Jesus' extraordinary power, the narrative of Jesus' arrest and death, and finally the story of the resurrection. Jesus himself told stories. Story has a power that a list of doctrines or an explanation of laws and beliefs simply doesn't have. That is because when we hear a story, we are drawn into the events narrated, we wait for something significant to happen. A good story always includes the promise of something interesting to come. A teacher who begins a lesson with "Boys and girls, let me tell you a story. . . ." may find much more rapt attention than would be the case if he or she began with "Boys and girls, let me explain transitive verbs."

The Gospels draw us into the story of Jesus. After a brief introduction, Luke begins his account—as we now have it—with "In the days of Herod, King of Judea, there was a priest. . . . " Luke imitated ancient storytelling language to draw his audience into the narrative. We are immediately transported into another time and place, and we wait for something to happen there.

Stories can bring us up short. They can surprise us, or reveal something about the emotions and thoughts of others that we never understood before. Stories can lead us beyond ourselves, beyond the limitations of our own imagining. Stories do not have to be "factual" to be true. There are profound truths in William Shakespeare's plays, even though the history he borrowed from is almost never factual. When we read a Gospel or even the Old Testament, we do not read it for factual history. The Bible is not a history book or a science text. It is a story of faith and includes narrative and poetic accounts of people who experienced the revelation of God.

Jesus told stories. The kind of stories he usually told are metaphoric narratives. They are realistic; that is, they are not fables. They are brief. They often have a double meaning. On the literal level, he could be talking about planting seeds; on the metaphoric level, he invites us to consider the vitality of the Word, how it grows, and what can keep it from growing.

Usually parables are not explained as clearly and as allegorically as the parable of the sower (*Mark 4:1–8; Matthew 13:1–9; Luke 8:4–8*). More often they end in a provocative or curiously surprising resolution, the kind of unsatisfying ending that often troubled the audience. Once Jesus told a story about someone being mugged and robbed and left dying beside the road. The only person who assisted him was a member of a despised ethnic group, a group considered the enemy by his listeners. The official religious leaders had passed by the victim, even crossing the road to avoid him. They were priests, for whom coming in contact with blood would have ritually defiled them. They would not have been able to offer sacrifice. We are used to this parable now, but we must transpose it into our own culture to understand the shock of this narrative. Jesus was speaking not only of love of neighbor, but also of the real meaning of sacrifice. His audience must have been confused by the story. By using a Samaritan as the example of a good neighbor, he altered the understanding of "good," as well as the understanding of "neighbor."

Sometimes the parables can be interpreted by their context in the Gospel, but more often the parable can suggest several interpretations. The point of a parable is not always precise because what is important is the interaction between the hearer and the revelation imbedded in the story. Our familiarity with many of the parables should not blind us to their relevance and to the serious questions they raise for our spiritual lives. The truth that they offer us is not in the category of "fact" but in the invitation to listen and to be changed.

Conversation

1. *Have you ever had the experience of reading Scripture and discovering a completely new meaning or understanding of the text? Explain.*

2. *Have the words of the Gospel ever troubled you? Explain.*

3. *How would you transpose the story of the Good Samaritan into contemporary culture?*

4. *We like to think that we would have listened and believed in Jesus and been instantly attracted to him. Do you think that would have been the case if you had experienced his presence in history? How do you think you would have responded?*

5. *Do we sentimentalize Jesus too much? What if he tells us something we do not want to hear? Has that ever happened to you? How can we respond?*

Silent Reflection/Journal Comments

I have strong feelings about certain aspects of my life and my religion. Is there any conviction that requires rethinking? What would it be? Are there people in my life or in my world that I have written off as morally hopeless? Who are they? Do I love them? How would I know that I love them?

Invitation to Conversion

A neighbor is someone who acts as a neighbor. The Good Samaritan acted as a neighbor. Act as a neighbor to someone you may have ignored.

Closing Prayer

Leader: Loving God, we thank you for your Word, your grace, your Spirit. We pray to you, who make all things new, to heal the wounds of the world.

All: O God, bring the healing of Christ to all who suffer, the light of Christ to our minds and hearts, and the peace of Christ to the world. We ask this in the name of our Lord, Jesus, who lives with you and the Holy Spirit now and always.

    Amen.

Social Time

Resource for Prayer in This Session

Lawton, Liam. *In the Quiet* (CD or cassette). GIA Publications, Inc.

Resources for Continued Growth

Crossan, John Dominic. *The Dark Interval: Towards a Theology of Story*. Sonoma, Calif.: Polebridge Press, 1988.

Tilley, Terence W. *Story Theology*. Wilmington, Del.: Michael Glazier, 1985.

Session 2

Jesus as Storyteller

Gathering Time

Overview

Jesus was the messenger of God to us. Without the example of his life, without his teaching, the meaning of his death and resurrection would be lost to us. Because he called into question long-standing cultural values and even religious ideas, his teaching was sometimes baffling to his listeners. He understood his audience quite well, however, and used their own value systems and customs to surprise them into a new understanding of God. Our familiarity with so many of his stories should not dull our own sense of astonishment at how different is the God he preached from what we consistently imagine, and how open our hearts must be to hear.

Focus

Because the teaching of Jesus challenged cultural values and religious ideas, his audience was sometimes offended. Some of the people were offended so much that they wished to kill him. The words of Jesus became a stumbling block, a scandal to those in authority whose power was threatened.

Opening Prayer

Leader: O God, be with us in our world, and open our eyes to see you where we live and work.

All: O God, be with us when we celebrate and when we suffer.

Leader: O God, look with compassion on the whole human family, unite us in the bonds of love. Through our struggle and confusion, lead us to your truth.

All: O God, be with us in your word and in your power.
Be with us as we search for truth.
How great is your love!
How wide is your mercy!
To you belong praise, glory, honor, and blessing forever.

Amen.

Group Reflection I: Jesus the Realist

Jesus was always aware of his audience. Like a good teacher, a good storyteller, or even a good parent, he understood the world of his listeners, and he wanted them to know that he understood that world. We don't have the exact words of Jesus, but we do have his voice, his persona. The Gospel writers testify to a man who was realistic, observant, and aware of the emotions of his listeners. They describe a man who was willing to debate, who was compassionate, who was sometimes troubled, who seemed on occasion to be exasperated or angry, and who wept in public.

According to Mark, the enemies of Jesus were quick to recognize his forthrightness: "Teacher, we know that you are a truthful man and that you are not concerned with anyone's opinion" (*Mark 12:14a*). This introduction to a test question may have been a ploy, a kind of setup for the question designed to trap Jesus: "Is it lawful to pay the census tax to Caesar or not?" (*Mark 12:14b*). Even if it was a setup, however, Jesus was not one to be taken by surprise. He knew about the tax, about the money, what it looked like, and who had it. Even if he was not carrying that money on his own person, he was well aware of its significance to those who were questioning him.

The parable of the ten gold coins in the Gospel of Luke (*Luke 19:11–27*) suggests that Jesus was aware of the value of money. He understood the laws of inheritance and the responsibilities of tenant farmers (*Luke 20:9–40)*. He knew about leaven and shepherds, vineyards and wine presses, patching clothes, table manners, the reputation of tax collectors, regional catastrophes, and the gossip about local sinners. He understood marriage customs, burial rites, cooking fish, planning a dinner, preparing the meal, and welcoming guests.

All of the Gospels testify to his familiarity with the household and civic life: from sweeping a house to the role of judges, and problem neighbors. *Luke 13:5* suggests that local news passed by word of mouth and Jesus was aware of what was happening around him. He had heard, for example, about the collapse of a tower near the old wall of the city and used the incident to make a point. (The victims were no more guilty than anyone else.) His speech was sometimes ironic ("A prophet is not without honor except in his native place and among his own kin and in his own house"—*Mark 6:4*), sometimes suggestive of exasperation ("O faithless and perverse generation, how long will I be with you and endure you?"—*Luke 9:41*), sometimes poignant ("Jerusalem, Jerusalem . . . I yearned to gather your children together, as a hen gathers her young under her wings"—*Matthew 23:37*). The evangelists give us a picture of a man of deep sensitivities, strong emotions, argumentative skill, and intense awareness of his mission from God.

His teaching was directed to an audience rooted in Middle Eastern culture and centuries of religious traditions. His task was to bring that audience from what they knew to what they might be able to imagine, and finally to convert his listeners to a new way of seeing. That meant disturbing preconceptions, dislodging familiar but stale ideas, sometimes shaking people's confidence in what they thought they knew, and even on occasion simply rebuking hostile interrogators. He was not afraid to offend, if offense was the only way to be faithful to his mission. In short, he was not always polite.

We have become so familiar with some of the Gospel scenes and we have seen so many biblical images in pious art that we may forget that the Gospel message can be just as disturbing to us as it surely was to the first generation of Christians. Jesus himself was disturbing, as Scripture reminds us. His actions and his words were parabolic; that is, they were not easily explained; they were culturally and politically subversive. As one Scripture scholar has argued, "The revolution that Jesus brings is liberation from those sociopolitical structures which deform people."[1] We do not easily attach ourselves to the words and actions of someone who challenges our cultural traditions. Often such people scandalize us. As St. Paul has written, however, the Cross itself is a scandal, a stumbling block (*1 Corinthians 1:23*). What does this word—*scandal*—mean in our spiritual lives? How does Jesus scandalize us?

Conversation

   1.   *How does the idea of Jesus as a realist affect your prayer life?*

---

[1]Terence W. Tilley, *Story Theology* (Wilmington, Del.: Michael Glazier, 1985), 114.

2. *Can you imagine Jesus saying anything to you that you would find upsetting?*

3. *What aspects of our culture are in conflict with the Gospel?*

4. *Do you think that the Gospel has affected culture in any way? Explain.*

5. *Are you disturbed by the use of power in economic, political, or ecclesiastical systems? How should we resist when systems, a workplace, or a person in power is unjust?*

Group Reflection II: The Meaning of a Scandal

In *Matthew 15:12*, the disciples are reported to have approached Jesus with the comment "Do you know that the Pharisees took offense when they heard what you said?" The Greek word for "took offense" is based on the word *scandal*. The Pharisees were scandalized by the words of Jesus. They were offended. Normally when we realize that we have offended someone, we rush to apologize. There is no indication in the text that Jesus was interested in apologizing. He knew he had offended his listeners. They had criticized him for not washing his hands. Jesus, in turn, criticized them for not obeying God's commandment to honor father and mother. He called attention to their abuse of the commandments. The Pharisees were managing to get around family obligations by a pious trick of dedicating their money to God. When Jesus criticized this longstanding custom among them, he was a "scandal" to them.

Another meaning of the word *scandal* in Greek is "stumbling block." *Skandalon* comes from *skadzo*, which means "I limp." In *Leviticus 19:14*, the Hebrews were reminded not to curse the deaf or put a stumbling block before the blind. In other words, to deceive an innocent person is to scandalize that person.

Similarly, Jesus reminds his listeners not to scandalize children (*Matthew 18:5*). They are innocent and easily deceived. They can be led astray because they cannot discern who is to be followed, who is to be imitated. Jesus turned on Peter on one occasion to say, "Get behind me, Satan! You are an obstacle [stumbling block, scandal] to me. You are thinking not as God does, but as human beings do" (*Matthew 16:23*). Clearly, this word *scandal* is rich in meaning. In the New Testament, it always refers to human beings who are a stumbling block to others. Peter was suggesting that Jesus should not suffer. His comment was understandable in human terms, but he was incapable at that time of grasping the full meaning of Jesus' passion and Jesus' willingness to deal with the consequences of his life and preaching.

Jesus was fully aware that his preaching and his mission would not be understood. He was fully aware that religious and civil authorities were unhappy with his views. He knew his words were offensive. He prayed, however, that there would be some who would not be scandalized by him, who would surrender their preconceptions about God and the Messiah and the way in which Israel would be redeemed. He prayed that some people would listen and give up their old ideas about a conquering Messiah who would help them throw off the yoke of the Romans. He praised those who could see beyond their immediate political and religious hopes to envision the reign of God in a new way: "And blessed is the one who takes no offense at me" *(Matthew 11:6; Luke 7:23)*.

What does it mean to be offended by Jesus? When anyone offends us, we react quickly because whatever was said or done did not correspond to our expectations of the other, or our own self-understanding. Discourtesy is offensive because we believe we should be treated with dignity. Someone has questioned our self-understanding or our values. To be scandalized or offended implies that one has certain expectations and convictions, and that those convictions are part of one's sense of self. If Jesus is described as saying, "Blessed is the one who takes no offense at me," he is suggesting that his words and actions may confront our self-understanding and perhaps our values—what we hold dear, what ideas we may not want to give up, what cultural traditions have become a kind of religion for us. Over fifty years ago, some Catholic parents rose up in social protest when Catholic schools were first integrated in the South. They picketed and resisted the determination of the bishop to integrate schools in New Orleans. The call of the Gospel for inclusion was so contrary to their cultural traditions that they were offended—scandalized. It was not the first time that the Gospel message came as a shock. Nor would it be the last.

Conversation

1. *Have you ever been irritated or troubled by the words of the Gospel?*

2. *Have you ever been simply confused by what Jesus seems to ask of us?*

3. *Think of a time when you were offended by someone. Can you explain why you were so pained? Was it failed expectation? Was it the shock that someone's opinion of you seemed so far from the truth? What was at stake?*

4. *Did you ever have to let go of a strong conviction? What led to the change of heart or mind? Why was it hard to let go? What was at stake?*

5. *Have you had the experience of suddenly realizing the implications of a scriptural passage for your own life? Comment on the circumstances.*

Silent Reflection/Journal Comments

When have I tried to ignore some aspect of the teaching of Christ? What was it I did not want to give up? some idea? some thing? What if Christ opened my mind and heart to suggest that I do something new, something I have never done before? How would I respond?

Invitation to Conversion

Let the other adult person win the argument. Don't insist on your idea or your preference or your theory. Give in.

Think of one cultural value that violates the Gospel and that pervades our society. How can you resist it?

Closing Prayer

All: Look with compassion, O God, on the people of our city and our land, especially those who live with injustice. Strengthen us to work for justice, to preach the Gospel in our world, to realize that no one is outside of your love. If our ears are closed, open them to hear your voice. If our eyes are shut, let them be open to your light. Hold us in your love forever.

    Amen.

Social Time

Resource for Prayer in This Session

Bell, John L., and the Iona Community. *One Is the Body* (CD or cassette). GIA Publications, Inc.

Resources for Continued Growth

Rohr, Richard. *Authentic Religion* (single audiocassettes). Cincinnati: St. Anthony Messenger Press, 2001.

Pilch, John. *The Cultural World of Jesus.* Cycle A. Collegeville, Minn.: The Liturgical Press, 1995.

Session **3**

The Future in Parables

Gathering Time

Overview

In preaching to us, Jesus used our ordinary concerns to reveal the extraordinary mercy of God. By proposing characters in his stories who closely resemble us and who reflect our own values, Jesus could open the hearers of the Word to a new understanding of God's values and God's kingdom. The parables of Jesus were designed to catch us by surprise, to alert us to what lies hidden from our view, and to imagine a God whose love surpasses what we ever imagined. If we think we understand our life, our future, and our relationship with God, perhaps Jesus has something to say to us that may be shocking.

Focus

Several parables emphasize the future: the future that we plan, the future for which we may be unprepared. As we plan for our own future—in history and beyond—we must consider what we desire most and what we are willing to sacrifice for our desires. Jesus urges us not to miscalculate.

Opening Prayer

Leader: O God, you alone know the future. You alone know the beauty of the treasure now hidden from our eyes. We do not ask you to keep us safe, but to give us courage so that we may be disciples of your Son.

All: Give us your wisdom and your grace.

Leader: From spiritual blindness . . .

All:	Lord, deliver us.
Leader:	From hardness of heart . . .
All:	Lord, deliver us.
Leader:	By your cross and suffering, by your death and resurrection . . .
All:	Lord, deliver us.
Leader:	Lord, you give us grace to read and hear your word. Help us to understand your teaching, to recognize the hidden treasure in your promises. Help us to understand what it means to be a disciple of your Son. We believe. Help our unbelief. We ask this in the name of your Son, Jesus Christ.
	Amen.

Group Reflection I: Counting the Cost

Two short parables in Luke—The Tower Builder (*14:28–30*) and The Warring King (*14:31–32*)—are about planning ahead. Of all the parables they are fairly simple, and they reveal Jesus' familiarity with matters that we usually don't associate with him: structural engineering and military strategy. A third parable, usually called The Treasure in the Field (*Matthew 13:44*), is more puzzling, although its general meaning seems clear enough. All three are instructions that address our tendency to focus on what is immediately important and to forget that the long-range goal is far more serious. Jesus says simply that anyone who wants to build a tower will calculate the cost before the building begins, lest the building remain half finished. Who wants to be laughed at for a conspicuous miscalculation? The warring king will calculate how many troops he will need before he sends them off to battle against the invaders. Perhaps it would be better to negotiate for peace immediately.

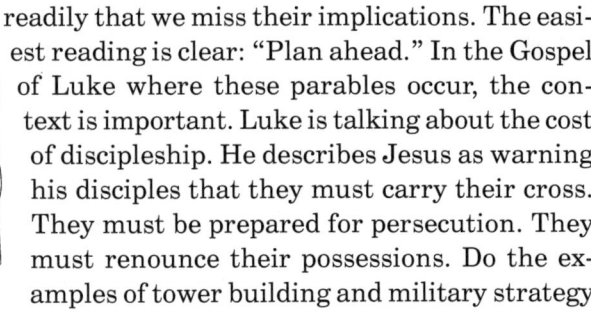

As simple as these parables seem, we cannot dismiss them so readily that we miss their implications. The easiest reading is clear: "Plan ahead." In the Gospel of Luke where these parables occur, the context is important. Luke is talking about the cost of discipleship. He describes Jesus as warning his disciples that they must carry their cross. They must be prepared for persecution. They must renounce their possessions. Do the examples of tower building and military strategy suggest that if we really calculate the cost, we may not want to make a commitment? The tower may never be built if it costs too much. The battle may never be fought and won. Or do the two parables suggest rather that most of us plan well when it comes to immediate problems but that the long-range goals are too often disregarded? Or is Jesus suggesting that when we respond to the call to be disciples, we must be aware of what the cost will be? These parables are not simple allegories. Their meaning is less obvious than we might suppose.

Jesus knew that our emotions and energies are often spent on immediate problems, and that we often plan quite well in order to resolve them. We may worry too much, in fact. Remember his comment about the lilies of the field? (*Matthew 6:28*) Was Jesus suggesting that we should work as hard at salvation as we work at paying the rent or building an addition to the house? Do we calculate our obligations to God with the same attention as we calculate the utility bills? What does it mean to calculate the cost of discipleship?

Matthew includes a parable of Jesus (*13:44*) about the kingdom of heaven that is related to the idea of cost. In this story, an unnamed person discovers that a treasure is hidden in a field. Joyfully realizing his good luck, he sells everything else that he owns so that he can buy the field. His audience, however, must have known that there was possibly something unethical about this behavior. The treasure really belonged to the property owner. Keeping the secret hidden from him may have been unjust. Are these details important to the meaning of the parable? What is Jesus suggesting about human craftiness? Would we sell everything that we have for the sake of purchasing the one thing that will bring us joy? Is that what the parable is about? What is it that we want that much? What are we willing to sacrifice for what we want?

Part of the force of the parable lies in its emphasis on the hiddenness of the treasure. No one seemed to know of its existence. In an earlier passage in this same chapter of Matthew's Gospel, Jesus describes himself as speaking in parables, announcing "what has lain hidden from the foundation [of the world]" (*Matthew 13:35*). So the treasure can mean many things. We do not know what lies hidden from us but is near us. We do not know how much joy that treasure could bring or what we must do to find and possess it. Jesus, however, wants to emphasize its value. A corresponding parable in this chapter speaks of a merchant who looks for and finds "a pearl of great price" (*Matthew 13:46*). He sells all that he has to buy it. And what will he do with one pearl? Was it worth the cost of selling everything else he had? How do we calculate the cost of any decision?

Conversation

1. *Have you ever made what you thought was a risky decision? How did you calculate the cost? What was at stake?*

2. *Have you ever had to "pay a price" for being Christian or for witnessing to the Gospel? Explain.*

3. *Have you ever had to give up something for the sake of doing what you knew to be God's will? Was it hard—or was it worth it? Explain.*

4. *The merchant who looked among pearls could recognize the one that was valuable. When we make choices about our lives and how we will spend our time and resources, how do we decide? How do we measure value?*

5. *Why does Jesus emphasize the* joy *of finding the treasure?*

Group Reflection II: What a Surprise!

When it comes to planning ahead, we think of retirement and enough income to support us in emergencies or in long-term care. It is normal to plan for our future. But when is our future? How far away is it? The parable of the rich fool (*Luke 12:16–21*) is a chilling reminder that the future moves in more rapidly than we sometimes realize. Here was a prosperous farmer whose harvest was so great that he decided to tear down his barns and build larger ones. He would store his grain, then rest, eat, drink, and be merry, for, as he said to himself, "you have so many good things stored up for many years." As the parable continues, God speaks: "You fool, this night your life will be demanded of you."

The question of the parable is not the fact of storing up things for oneself, but rather, not storing up "what matters to God." In the context of the Gospel where this parable is found, Jesus is responding to a question about inheritance. A man in the crowd wants his brother to share the inheritance with him. The parable of the rich fool functions partly as a response to the problem. "Take care to guard against all greed," Jesus had said before telling the parable (*Luke 12:15*).

But it is not just greed that is the rich fool's problem. It is his complacency and self-centeredness. He seems to be aware only of himself and his personal success. The parable doesn't suggest that financial security is bad or that planning for financial security is bad. The parable is about other moral problems that can accompany our eagerness for security. The parable ends with a curious question: "[A]nd the things you have prepared, to whom will they belong?" That question is left hanging. Who will own the harvest? Who already owns the harvest? We can plan and plan and forget the one thing necessary, or forget that we may never have the kind of future for which we had been preparing.

The parable of the prodigal son (*Luke 15:11–32*) is so rich in meaning, and such a classic symbol of the God preached by Jesus that all the homilies we have ever heard seem not to have exhausted its depth. We can reflect on the two brothers, one faithful and dutiful, the other irresponsible and self-indulgent; we can consider the shock of asking for the inheritance before the death of the father; the degradation into which the wayward son fell (taking care of pigs, the most unclean of animals for a devout Jew); and the speech that the prodigal had prepared to recite but never could—because his father was too filled with joy to listen. We can even think of the servants who never have a word to say but were told to bear a message of forgiveness to someone who didn't want to hear it.

Forgiveness, joy, repentance, resentment—the parable is filled with human emotions. The meaning of scandal is built into the parable. It is the elder brother who is scandalized. By what? By the father's willingness, even eagerness, to forgive. The father watches and waits, then runs to greet his wayward son. The goodness of the father becomes a stumbling block for the faithful son. Unfathomable goodness turned the elder son from a dutiful servant into a man seething with resentment, a brother who refuses to celebrate with his returning relative. "Your son," he says to the father, rather than "my brother" (*Luke 15:30*). This narrative, which seems clearly to point to the God of Jesus, should force us to reflect on whether or not God's universal and infinitely forgiving love is ever a scandal to us.

Perhaps we should confess that we understand the elder brother's feelings. We suspect that he has earned his father's love and that the foolish son has not. Are we scandalized then by the realization that love cannot be earned? When the father pleads with his elder son to come and celebrate, we do not know how he responded, but as Scripture scholar John Dominic Crossan has observed, "in the end the parable shows a prodigal son inside feasting and a dutiful son outside pouting."[1] This is an example of the unexpected reversal that characterizes the reign of God in the preaching of Jesus. In the beginning of chapter 15 where this parable occurs, Luke writes: "The tax collectors and sinners were all drawing near to listen to him, but the Pharisees and scribes began to complain, saying, 'This man welcomes sinners and eats with them'" (*Luke 15:1*). The openness and hospitality of Jesus had scandalized respectable people. The result was a transformation. Respectable people became disrespectful, critical, and resentful, and sinners became publicly respectable. Jesus himself was becoming a scandal.

Conversation

1. *If we try hard to do God's will, to grow in the spiritual life, how do we feel about those who seem utterly indifferent to God and to morality—whose actions strike us as vulgar and stupid?*

2. *Do our relatives or friends sometimes seem completely unworthy of our trust and affection? How do we respond to them if favors are asked?*

3. *How will the prodigals of this world discover the love and forgiveness of God?*

4. *Will we be surprised to know who eats and drinks with Jesus in the kingdom? Explain.*

5. *Why do good people sometimes become unpleasant, critical, and judgmental? What is the problem?*

Silent Reflection/Journal Comments

What am I willing to give up for the sake of being a disciple? Is there anything I am willing to die for? What? What do I live for every day? Why?

Invitation to Conversion

Doctors sometimes advise patients whose illness is terminal to "get their affairs in order." Consider any spiritual affairs that you need to get in order if you were told that you had only a few weeks to live. Should you reconcile with anyone? forgive anyone? Who needs to be told of your love? Is there anything you need to sacrifice for the sake of the "pearl of great price"?

[1]John Dominic Crossan, *In Parables* (New York: Harper and Row, 1973), 74.

Closing Prayer

Leader: Let us celebrate the goodness of God.

All: Happy those whose help is Jacob's God,
whose hope is in the LORD, their God,
The maker of heaven and earth,
the seas and all that is in them,
Who keeps faith forever,
secures justice for the oppressed,
gives food to the hungry.
The LORD sets prisoners free;
the LORD gives sight to the blind.

—Psalm 146:5–8a

Blessed be the name of the Lord.

Social Time

Resource for Prayer in This Session

Paul, Susan J. *We Will Remember* (CD or cassette). GIA Publications, Inc.

Resources for Continued Growth

Keating, Thomas. *The Kingdom of God Is Like*. New York: Crossroad Publishing Company, 1993.

Reid, Barbara A. *Parables for Preachers: The Gospel of Luke, Year C*. Collegeville Minn.: The Liturgical Press, 2000.

———. *Parables for Preachers: The Gospel of Matthew, Year A*. Collegeville, Minn.: The Liturgical Press, 2001.

The Unexpected in Parables

Gathering Time

Overview

Jesus understands people quite well. He knows our desires, our goodness, our not-so-goodness, and our constant habit of comparing ourselves with others. He calls us to self-knowledge, humility, and a willingness to look to God for our reputation and our reward, not to anyone else. His parables suggest that we should work as hard at our salvation as we work at earning a living.

Focus

When we see the depth of the goodness of God, we may well be astonished. Measuring ourselves by the goodness or the failures of others, trying to measure God's mercy, claiming privileges, and assuming that we know God's opinions are all dangerous spiritual attitudes. Jesus alerts us to these dangers.

Opening Prayer

Leader: I raise my eyes toward the mountains.
        From where will my help come?
   My help comes from the LORD,
        the maker of heaven and earth.

All: God will not allow your foot to slip;
        your guardian does not sleep.
   Truly, the guardian of Israel
        never slumbers nor sleeps.
   The LORD is your guardian;
        the LORD is your shade
        at your right hand.

Leader:	By day the sun cannot harm you,
	nor the moon by night.
	The LORD will guard you from all evil,
	will always guard your life.
All:	The Lord will guard your coming and going
	both now and forever.

—Psalm 121:1–8

Leader: O God, keep our eyes fixed on you. Help us to see ourselves in your light. Help us to remember your mercy, and let go of our hardness of heart. Our help comes from you. Never let us go. We ask this in the name of your Son, our Lord.

Amen.

Group Reflection I: The Back of the Line

"The kingdom of heaven is like a landowner who went out at dawn to hire laborers for his vineyard" (*Matthew 20:1*).

If we were asked to describe the way we picture heaven, would we begin with a line like this? In many cities of the world, especially in the Middle East, this scene is quite familiar. Day laborers gather in a designated street corner or lot, hoping that a truck or bus will come along whose driver has work orders for so many fruit pickers or other agricultural workers. They will be returned to the street corner at the end of the day. So how is this like the kingdom of heaven?

Here the scandal begins. Having agreed to work for a day's wages, workers are shocked to see that the employer offers a day's wages to those who had just started to work at the end of the day. Offended by what seems an obvious injustice, they begin complaining until the employer argues, "Did you not agree with me for the usual daily wage? Take what is yours and go. . . . [A]m I not free to do as I wish with my own money? Are you envious because I am generous?" (*Matthew 20:13–15*) The parable ends with "Thus, the last will be first, and the first will be last" (*20:16*). Literary scholar David McCracken comments: "Human institutions are posited on the reverse: the first will be first, and the last, last. It is common sense, it is the way things are . . . but the kingdom of heaven that Jesus is talking about has nothing to do with common sense; nothing to do with the ordinary way things are on earth, though everything to do with the way things are or shall be in the kingdom of heaven. . . ."[1]

[1]David McCracken, *The Scandal of the Gospels: Jesus, Story, and Offense* (New York: Oxford University Press, 1994), 79.

The reader or hearer of this text, familiar with the ways things are here on earth, is as offended perhaps as the twelve-hour workers. We are offended because common sense doesn't seem to apply. Reasoning doesn't seem to work. And it is here that our faith is challenged. This is not to say that God is irrational. (We cannot simply identify the landowner with God.) It is to say that we cannot apply our standards to God. The story forces us to let go of our usual way of thinking. We can be scandalized by the story and end up grumbling—like the workers transformed into sulks—or we can open ourselves to possibility. Faith can begin with letting go of some of our presuppositions and allowing ourselves to be transformed into believing disciples.

Part of the difficulty of the workers who complained was their sense of entitlement. That same perspective is at issue in the parable of the places of honor at a wedding banquet. "[D]o not recline at table in the place of honor. A more distinguished guest than you may have been invited" (*Luke 14:8*). In this story, the guest may be obliged to take a lower place. Why not begin with the lowest place and then be asked to move up? suggests Jesus. In one sense, this is mere calculation. If I pretend to be humble, then I will be exalted. If this were the point, then the parable is merely about honor and shame. What should I do to make sure that I will never be shamed? But Jesus is using a fairly rigid custom to make another point. How should we see ourselves at the banquet in the kingdom of God? Who is invited to the table? Who decides the place of honor? the guests? They could be mistaken. If we have been invited, our standards may be reversed by the one who has invited us.

A surprising reversal characterizes the parable of the Pharisee and the tax collector (*Luke 18:9–14*). Reading this parable of the morally upright Pharisee and the sinful outcast, we must not oversimplify the scene. The difference is not between good people and sinners. The problem is good people who are proud of their moral standing before God and whose pride is based on comparing themselves with others. If the Pharisee had compared himself with the holiness of God, had measured himself by standards other than human comparisons, his self-understanding would have been quite different.

The tax collector knew he was not entitled to the mercy of God, and he "went home justified" (*Luke 18:14*). The difference between the two men is their sense of entitlement. If we think we are earning our way to heaven, we should probably think again. God's ways are not our ways. In the presence of God, what can we say we are entitled to?

Conversation

1. *If you work hard to be good all your life, do you believe you are entitled to a heavenly reward? Why or why not?*

2. *Do you ever hear people complain about God? What is the basis of their criticism?*

3. *Do you ever find yourself in the business of comparing? (Are there people who are more immoral or unethical than you? Or do you think God loves other people more than God loves you?) Are such comparisons inevitable? What is the effect of such comparisons on your relationship to God?*

4. *Do you ever feel that some people just don't deserve mercy? Who? Why?*

5. *Have the religious ideas of other people ever angered you? Why? Where do people get their ideas about religion? about God? Where is God in this kind of dispute?*

Group Reflection II: Getting It Right

One of the surprising elements of Jesus' storytelling is his use of ordinary, even unethical and calculating people to reveal something about the mystery of God's kingdom. The parable of the persistent widow—sometimes called the story of the unjust judge—is a case in point. We don't know why or how the judge is unjust. We only know, by his own admission, that he "neither feared God nor respected any human being" (*Luke 18:2*). The contradiction between his work and his ethics is enough to remind us that the widow will have a hard time. But she is persistent. "[T]his widow keeps bothering me," he concludes. "I shall deliver a just decision for her lest she finally come and strike me" (*Luke 18:5*). According to Scripture scholar Barbara Reid, the English translation actually softens her threat. In Greek the line reads, "lest she give me a black eye."[2]

These two interesting characters are not exactly typical, either in Jewish culture or in our own. But there they are in Jesus' story,

[2]Barbara Reid, *Parables for Preachers: The Gospel of Luke, Year C* (Collegeville, Minn.: The Liturgical Press, 2000), 231.

used to make a point. The easiest reading of this curious scenario is not the only way to understand it. Is Jesus saying simply that we should persevere in prayer? But the unjust judge is not a very helpful representative of God, who always hears the cry of the widow. Besides, if the judge doesn't fear either God or human beings, why should he fear a poor widow? He simply wants to get rid of her. Jesus' audience would be puzzled by this story and its characters who do not fit their cultural stereotypes. Jesus may have wanted to jar their other stereotypes—especially their stereotypical view of God. This parable asks us to wrestle with unfamiliar notions about God. It alerts us, moreover, to the kind of struggle we must undertake to find justice in an unjust world.[3]

Another ungenerous character described in *Luke 11:5–8* wants to stay in bed when his neighbor is banging on the door. The neighbor has an unexpected visitor and no food in the house. The persistence of the neighbor finally roused him, even when friendship didn't. Here Jesus uses the most ordinary characters and the most ordinary situation to emphasize the extraordinary power of prayer. His familiarity with these human dilemmas reminds us that our own human dilemmas can be parabolic. Jesus could have used any of the little tragedies and sitcoms in our lives—the awkward situations, the embarrassing incidents, or the irritating neighbors— to tell us something about God, as well as something about divine friendship.

One of the reasons the parables are scandalous is that Jesus uses such unpleasant people to tell us about God. If there is any parable that typifies this style of preaching, it is surely the parable of the unjust steward (*Luke 16:1–8*). Knowing that he was going to be fired for misusing money, the steward altered the books so that his employer would not know how much he was owed by his debtors. He did so in order to ingratiate himself with the debtors. He knew he would need friends. In the parable, the unjust steward is praised by his employer for acting prudently. We cannot imagine a more puzzling scenario: an employer praising an employee for engaging in what looks like fraud in order to save his own neck. What are we to make of this story, especially since so much is left unexplained?

We need not research the business customs of the first century to sense that the steward was cunning enough to save himself. Forgiveness of debts was one way to do it. Is this story an example of

[3]Reid, *Parables for Preachers*, 233.

the deep irony of Jesus who notes that the "children of this world" are more prudent than the children of light? Unrighteous people can be clever—even hard-working—in order to achieve their goals—whether they plot to rob a bank or embezzle funds from their clients and employers. Perhaps they work even harder at achieving their goals than others who work for more worthy causes. Is Jesus suggesting that the unrighteous can be models for us? It could be argued that he was being a little offensive. Unjust judges, clamoring widows, cunning stewards, grumbling neighbors—these portrayals of human beings are not particularly flattering. Jesus could point to these rough relationships, however, and to our own unrighteousness to tell us about God.

Conversation

1. *If Jesus were to preach today, do you think he would offend some people? How?*

2. *How hard is it for us to "get it right" about God? Do you think many of us misunderstand God completely? Do you think our ideas about God are a little stale?*

3. *Has preaching ever disturbed you or shaken your ideas about God? Explain.*

4. *What is the advantage of being a little confused about God and God's ways?*

5. *Can you cite any examples of violent and cruel people working hard at their jobs? sacrificing completely in order to advance their own cause? Do we work that hard at advancing the cause of peace? Is there a parable here?*

Silent Reflection/Journal Comments

When is the last time I compared myself with someone else? What was the effect of this reflection on my own self-understanding? Can I let go of resentment? How?

Invitation to Conversion

Be persistent in working for justice. What unjust situation in your city or the world calls for your attention and concern? Write a letter. Make a contribution. Join the group struggling to resolve that situation. Help the next person who asks you for support and assistance.

Closing Prayer

Leader: Our help is in the name of the Lord
Who made heaven and earth.

All: Give us, O God, reverence for the truth—
The truth about ourselves,
The truth about justice and injustice.
Give us the desire both to think and to speak truly.
Save us from the fear of others, from the fear of
self-knowledge.
Direct us in all that we do, that in all of our lives,
in all of our work,
We may praise you.

Leader: We lift our eyes to you, O Lord, in whom is our salvation. You are light when all is dark. In you we see light. In you is the truth that frees us from fear and gives us hope. We believe in you, we hope in you, we ask for mercy in the name of your Son, Jesus.

Amen.

Resource for Prayer in This Session

Haugen, Marty, with Gary Daigle. *The Feast of Life: Stories from the Gospel of Luke* (CD or cassette). GIA Publications, Inc.

Resources for Continued Growth

Donahue, J. R. *The Gospel in Parable: Metaphor, Narrative, and Theology in the Synoptic Gospels.* Philadelphia: Fortress Press, 1988.

Green, B. *Like a Tree Planted: An Exploration of Psalms and Parables through Metaphor.* Collegeville, Minn.: The Liturgical Press, 1997.

Session 5

Parables of Judgment

Gathering Time

Overview

The concern we direct to possible danger in our lives should remind us that we should be equally concerned about our spiritual destiny. Assuming that Christ's coming into our lives is a long way off—or a distant dream—is to misread the Gospel. Christ's presence is real; his coming is inevitable. Even when we are preoccupied with our own daily problems or the violence and injustice of the world around us, we must make visible in our world the mercy and love of Christ. We must see in the brokenness of our world the Christ who suffers.

Focus

The parables of judgment remind us of how important it is to stay spiritually awake, to prepare ourselves to meet Christ, whose coming may surprise us, whose presence may be concealed in the suffering of our neighbor.

Opening Prayer

Leader: You who dwell in the shelter of the Most
      High
    who abide in the shadow in the Almighty
Say to the LORD, "My refuge and my fortress,
    my God in whom I trust."

All: God's faithfulness is a protecting shield.

Leader: You have the LORD for your refuge;
    you have made the Most High your
      stronghold.
No evil shall befall you. . . .

All: For God commands the angels
   to guard you in all your ways.

Leader: Whoever clings to me I will deliver;
   whoever knows my name I will set on
    high.

All: All who call upon me I will answer;
   I will be with them in distress;
   I will deliver them and give them honor.
 With length of days I will satisfy them
   and show them my saving power.
      —*Psalm 91:1–2, 4b, 9–10a, 11, 14–16*

Leader: Lord, grant that we may draw joy from your word.
   Keep us in your peace. Draw us to yourself. Give us
   the gift of remembering your word, treasuring it in
   our hearts, and proclaiming it by our words and
   actions so that the Gospel may heal the world.

All: Amen.

Group Reflection I: Staying Awake

Judging from the stories he told, Jesus was very much aware of all kinds of unscrupulous and unpleasant people in his society: grumblers, embezzlers, the violent, the foolish, the self-important, and the public sinners. He knew that money had to be hidden, that servants could not always be trusted, that people could be left dying and unattended on the side of the road. He used the caution of the ordinary citizen to stretch our imaginations and to alert us to another kind of reality, another necessary caution. He compared himself to a thief (*Matthew 24:43–44*).

What do thieves do? They wait for darkness. They wait until their victims are asleep. They try to take advantage of the element of surprise. "Be sure of this: if the master of the house had known the hour of night when the thief was coming, he would have stayed awake and not let his house be broken into." We cannot allegorize this warning to suggest that Jesus is just waiting until we are unprepared before snatching us into eternity. That is clearly not the point. But comparing the Son of Man to a thief is startling. We do prepare for the possibility of thieves and burglars. We lock our doors; we clutch our purses to our side; we conceal our money. Jesus knew that villagers of his own day were equally cautious. He also knew that if we are warned, we are doubly prepared. So here is the warning: "[A]t an hour you do not expect, the Son of Man will come" (*Matthew 24:44*).

Most of us do not like surprises like this. Sudden death, sudden calamities, the end of the world. Let's confess: we try not to think about these things. Avoidance of these matters helps our peace of mind. In Matthew's Gospel especially, Jesus asks us to think ahead. Death and judgment may indeed come suddenly—like a thief in the night. If the thought makes us a little uncomfortable, perhaps this parable has achieved its purpose. A little discomfort is better than complacency.

Another parable speaks to the same issue. Some people are prepared to meet Jesus, some, apparently, are not. The parable of the ten young virgins (sometimes called bridesmaids) is complex in its cultural setting, but not that difficult to link to the problem of the thief in the night. "[T]he kingdom of heaven will be like ten virgins who took their lamps and went out to meet the bridegroom" (*Matthew 25:1*). But the bridegroom was "long delayed." The next twelve verses tell us that all of the girls fell asleep, but five of them had prepared for a possible delay and had purchased enough oil for their lamps to keep them burning. The others had not. When their oil ran out, they left to purchase more. In the meantime, the bridegroom arrived, escorted five girls into the wedding party, and locked the door to the others. "I do not know you," he said, when they wanted in. If this doesn't make us uncomfortable, the parable hasn't worked at all.

The poor girls weren't bad people, after all. They were just a little careless. They didn't plan ahead. Isn't the bridegroom being rather harsh? Who is this bridegroom? Is Jesus talking about himself? Doesn't Jesus always open the door to those who knock? We should probably face the fact that this parable was not designed to make us feel good. Our discomfort should lead us to think about its implications.

The long delay before we see the coming of the Son of Man, the long delays in our lives before we realize that our eternal destiny is at stake, may lead us to fall asleep. The Gospel writers are uncomfortable about anyone's falling asleep. This somnolent state suggests that we are not spiritually aware, that we are not ready to meet the Lord at his coming. How well do these parables of watching and waiting jar us into a different frame of mind?

Conversation

1. *It has been said that the five young women simply failed to realize the situation. How can an oversight like this be spiritually or morally disastrous?*

2. *What does spiritual preparedness mean? If you knew that your life would end tomorrow, would you stop everything and pray? Why or why not?*

3. *Some religions focus their spirituality on the end of the world. What are the advantages and disadvantages of this emphasis?*

Group Reflection II: What Then?

We do not know when the end of the world will happen or how. In the meantime, we have our own moment in history in which to live. We would like to think that after Jesus, evil gradually diminished and that the Spirit of Jesus converted millions and millions of people to love of neighbor. Evil, however, is very much with us, and, for many, the presence of evil is the greatest obstacle to belief in God. Addressing this perennial issue, Jesus offered a remarkable parable: "The kingdom of heaven may be likened to a man who sowed good seed in his field. While everyone was asleep his enemy came and sowed weeds all through the wheat . . . " (*Matthew 13:24–25*). We are told that the weeds in question were darnel, whose poisonous leaves emit a toxin. The situation occurred "when everyone was asleep," an element of the story we should not overlook. The slaves of the householder are rightly puzzled: "[D]id you not sow good seed in your field?" (*Matthew 13:27*)

The householder, however, knows immediately that "an enemy has done this" (*Matthew 13:28*). The obvious solution, according to those familiar with the agricultural crisis—and presumably Jesus' audience—is to pull up the weeds immediately. The surprise occurs when the householder instructs the slaves to wait until the harvest. The householder is unhappy about the weeds, but he knows that the wheat is not in danger. At the harvest—always a metaphor in Matthew for the end of the world—everything will be pulled up, and the wheat and the weeds will then be separated.

We are so familiar with this parable that it may not startle us anymore. But it was meant to surprise us. Good gardeners do not tolerate weeds. Good farmers do not sit back and watch them grow, especially since the harvest is a long way away. We can admit that we are surrounded by weeds. And they are toxic. We are like the slaves who turn to the householder with the puzzled query: "Why do you let these things happen? Why don't you do something about it? Where were you? Just because we are asleep, it doesn't follow that you should be sleeping. We're going to take care of this right now."

There is something a little irritating about the householder saying to us, "No, if you pull up the weeds you might uproot the wheat along with them. Let them grow together . . ."(*Matthew 13:29–30*). So we are left with the weeds and a householder who is more patient than we—at least for the moment.

We should also consider the sheep and the goats in Matthew's great climactic scene of judgment (*Matthew 25: 31–46*). In this stunning narrative, moral and ethical disputes are resolved into one criterion: mercy. "[W]hatever you did for one of these least brothers of mine, you did for me" (*Matthew 25:40*). One of the problems of the parable is that even the sheep and goats don't know which is which. They are all surprised at the end: "[W]hen did we see you?" (*Matthew 25:37*) Perhaps that should tell us something about ourselves and others in this moment of history before the judgment.

Matthew's two parables of judgment usually remind us of the end of the world, but that is probably not their purpose. Both parables suggest something about the present and about the mixture of good and evil in history. They suggest that it is not always easy to distinguish between what is good and what is not—that we must be cautioned not to pull up weeds without the householder's authorization. After all, we could be mistaken. British theologian James Alison comments on this parable: "This is in no way a description of a future gathering beyond the grave. The criterion for judgment is already present in the midst of the world; we do not have to wait until later."[1] Those who are not scandalized by what looks like a toxic plant, or by the poor and hungry and marginalized of this world have "already passed through judgment."[2]

Conversation

1. *Does the presence of evil in the world disturb your faith? Why or why not?*

2. *Some Christians are militant in their condemnation of evil and evil people in the world. Comment.*

3. *Do the parables suggest that there is nothing we should do about evil in the world? Comment.*

4. *What does James Alison mean when he writes, "The criterion for judgment is already present in the midst of the world?"*

[1]James Alison, *Raising Abel: The Recovery of the Eschatological Imagination* (New York: Crossroad Publishing Company, 1996), 157.

[2]Ibid.

Silent Reflection/Journal Comments

What evil have I experienced in my life, and how have I responded to it? How have I balanced mercy and judgment in my relations with others? What people in my life have I criticized perhaps too harshly? How can I temper my attitude towards them?

Invitation to Conversion

Who in your city or among your associates and friends is the most abandoned? How can you address their problems? Contribute to a battered women's shelter, or arrange to assist imprisoned women. Your diocese provides for many social service structures. Volunteer to assist one of them.

Closing Prayer

Leader: Look with compassion, O God, upon the people of our city and our world who live with injustice, terror, disease, and death. Have mercy on us and those given us to love.

All: O God, no one is beyond the reach of your love
   or your mercy.
Be with us as we try to love.
Be with us as we try to serve.
Move and inspire us to see with your eyes.
Give us strength of purpose and concern for others
That we may create a community and a world
   of justice and of peace.

Leader: We turn to you, O God, in our longing to see clearly and to love courageously.
Fill our hearts with your own love and mercy. We ask this through our Lord Jesus Christ, your Son.
Amen.

Social Time

Resource for Prayer in This Session

Haugen, Marty. *Gift of God* (CD or cassette). GIA Publications, Inc.

Resources for Continued Growth

Gowler, David B. *What Are They Saying about the Parables?* New York: Paulist Press, 2000.

Herzog, William R., II. *Parables as Subversive Speech: Jesus as Pedagogue of the Oppressed*. Louisville: Westminster/John Knox Press, 1994.

Hoppe, Leslie. *A Retreat with Matthew*. Cincinnati: St. Anthony Messenger Press, 2000.

Session 6

The Scandal of the Cross

Gathering Time

Overview

The life and death of Jesus, as well as his teaching, was and remains a stumbling block to those who hear the Gospel. The subversion of all the usual cultural values—victory, success, wealth, reputation, security—was and continues to be an obstacle to belief. To accept the Gospel is not irrational, but it does require letting go of values we often hold dear and of goods for which we struggle. It means letting go of some of our most cherished opinions—of ourselves and of others. To accept the Gospel means that we have not been scandalized by Jesus and the Abba he reveals to us. To accept the Gospel is to admit finally that we do not understand all of its implications but that we are willing to follow and to wait and to believe that the kingdom of God is a hidden treasure. To possess that treasure, we must sell all that we have.

Focus

Many of the parables try to prepare us for the complete reversal of our expectations. The teaching of Jesus is transmitted to us so that we can be prepared for the cross, so that we can learn to let go of our impoverished expectations and hope in the God who surprises us. The cross itself could not prepare us for the resurrection. The God that Jesus preached comes to us always as the surprise of our life.

Opening Prayer

Leader: Loving God, you sent your Son, Jesus Christ, to announce the Good News of the kingdom.

His life, his mission, his death and resurrection
proclaimed your goodness and mercy, your love for all
creation and for all men and women.

All: We bless the Lord, the God of Israel,
for he has visited and brought redemption to his
people.
He has given us knowledge of salvation through the
forgiveness of sins.

Leader: We bless the Lord our God.

All: We bless the Lord our God
because of his tender mercy
by which the daybreak from on high will visit us

Leader: To shine on those who sit in darkness
and death's shadow,
To guide our feet into the path of peace.

All: We bless the Lord our God now and forever.
Amen.

Group Reflection I: Coming in Last

"[B]lessed is the one who takes no offense at me" (*Matthew 11:6*).
This beatitude in Matthew's Gospel is a commentary on the teaching and the life of Jesus. It could be translated "Blessed is the one
who is not scandalized by me." Jesus was aware that many who
heard him turned away in disbelief and that others found his teaching puzzling, if not incomprehensible. Luke, who often uses meals
and dining as a metaphor for the Christian life, includes a story
known as the parable of the great supper (*Luke 14:15–24*). When we
hear it today, we are as puzzled as Jesus' hearers. If it contradicted
the values of a first-century audience, we cannot argue that our values are that much different.

In this story, a rich man prepared a great dinner to which those
invited excused themselves for reasons that seem like fabricated
excuses to get out of the social event. One has purchased a field,
another has to check on his oxen, and another just got married. The
excuses seem reasonable enough—as are most of our excuses—but
the rich man becomes angry. He sends his servants to the streets
and the alleys and orders the poor, the crippled, the blind, and the
lame to come. The servant is then sent out to the highways and
hedgerows. The house is to be full of people celebrating. The parable ends with "I tell you, none of those men who were invited will
taste my dinner" (*Luke 14:24*). His audience knew that the parable

alluded to the kingdom of God. Someone in the audience had started the discussion with the comment "Blessed is the one who will dine in the kingdom of God." (*Luke 14:15*). But what were people to think of the final observation: None of those originally invited will taste the dinner.

This subversion of the typical celebration, this startling comment that all sorts of unwanted and undesirable people will be celebrating while the merchants and landowners are off doing business, echoes a common theme in the Gospels: "The last shall be first." (See *Luke 13:30*; *Matthew 19:30; Mark 9:35,10:31.*) Scripture scholar John Dominic Crossan comments: "'Can you imagine,' asks Jesus, 'a situation in which all the invited guests are absent from a banquet and all the uninvited ones are present?' . . . [T]his invites the hearers to recognize a situation of total reversal. As a parable it provokes their response to the Kingdom's arrival as radical and absolute reversal of their closed human situation."[1]

Our familiarity with the Gospel texts should not dull us to the implications of such a parable. Jesus often subverts those values we consider most fundamental. He warns us that we may live within "a closed situation" that needs to be examined.

The total reversal of the parables parallels the total reversal that characterized the death of Jesus. That his disciples were unwilling to acknowledge the possibility of such a reversal is clear from Jesus' rebuke to Peter. When Peter resists the possibility of Jesus' arrest and execution, Jesus invokes the word *scandal*. In some translations, Jesus is described as saying "Get behind me, Satan! You are an obstacle to me" (*Matthew 16:23*). "Obstacle," in this translation of *skandalon*, indicates clearly that Peter is in his way. Jesus continues, "You are thinking not as God does, but as human beings do." Jesus must go on his way, the way of the cross. This was not the future that Peter and the disciples envisioned. Nor is it the way anyone in history could imagine how to attract followers. That the cross would be a stumbling block was clearly a possibility. Jesus died a criminal's death, and the manner of his death was a problem from the beginning.

Is there anyone who really looks forward to taking up the cross?

Was there a single disciple who was prepared for the resurrection?

---

[1]John Dominic Crossan, *In Parables* (New York: Harper and Row, 1973), 73.

Conversation

1. *Can you think of common human values or desires that we need to reexamine for their relationship to the Gospel?*

2. *How would Jesus comment on the frequently heard expression at a sports event: "We're number 1!" Can you imagine a parable based on that expression?*

3. *Can you imagine inviting "street people" to your home for a big dinner? Why or why not?*

4. *How does the parable of the great supper relate to the principle of inclusiveness in neighborhoods, churches, schools, and workplaces?*

Group Reflection II: The Stone Rejected

In Luke's Gospel, Jesus is described as telling a parable about a man who leased his vineyard to tenant farmers. At harvest time, he sent his servants to collect produce. The tenant farmers killed his servants, one after another, and finally killed even the man's son. Jesus describes the anger of the man who decides to put the tenant farmers to death and lease the land to others (*Luke 20:9–19*). This parable is followed by a quotation from *Psalm 118*: "The stone the builders rejected/ has become the cornerstone" (*118:22*).

Jesus asks his listeners to explain the scriptural passage. Then he adds, "Everyone who falls on that stone will be dashed to pieces; and it will crush anyone on whom it falls" (*Luke 20:18*). This is metaphor at its most difficult. His listeners, however, recognized a warning. The text continues: "The scribes and chief priests sought to lay their hands on him at that very hour . . . " (*Luke 20:19*).

Another passage in the New Testament makes the link between the words of Jesus and the scandal of his arrest and execution. "Come to him, a living stone, rejected by human beings but chosen and precious in the sight of God" (*1 Peter 2:4*). The writer links this stone to the idea of scandal or stumbling block: It is "'A stone that will make people stumble,/ and a rock that will make them fall.'/ They stumble by disobeying the word . . . " (*1 Peter 2:8*).

The cross, as St. Paul and many others have pointed out, is the supreme scandal. Not only was the death of Jesus disgraceful and ignominious, but also it was and remains a scandal for deeper reasons. It reveals what happens when human beings are obsessed by their own version of God, their own vision of themselves, and their violent mechanisms for expelling those who challenge that vision.

The cross is a scandal because it reveals a God who is radically different from the God we had imagined. This is a God whose messenger forgives us even as we set out to expel him from the world. This Jesus spoke of God as his Father, his Abba. Listening to him, his hearers—then and now—struggle to believe. This God Jesus revealed is not the God most of us had in mind, not even the God we wanted.

If we were to write the script for someone who would be the messenger and mediator of God in human history, this is not the script we would have written. We were not prepared for this kind of human being, this kind of message. Jesus was an offense to many of his listeners. He was an offense to the Roman authorities. He disappointed his followers. His spirituality and religion were not success-oriented. He was not interested in money, fame, popularity, tranquillity, or personal security. He offended powerful people, scandalized the pious, and bewildered those who loved him. Jesus knew how he would be received. He was not naive. He knew that his followers would be tempted to give up completely, to resist the mission they had been assigned, and to run away from the consequences of preaching his word.

"I have told you this," he said before his death, "so that you may not fall away [so that you will not be offended—scandalized]" (*John 16:1*). So we should be prepared. St. Paul warns us also: He speaks of the cross as "foolishness," as a "stumbling block."

> Has not God made the wisdom of the world foolish? For since in the wisdom of God the world did not come to know God through wisdom, it was the will of God through the foolishness of the proclamation to save those who have faith. For Jews demand signs and Greeks look for wisdom, but we proclaim Christ crucified, a stumbling block to Jews and foolishness to Gentiles. . . . For the foolishness of God is wiser than human wisdom, and the weakness of God is stronger than human strength (*1 Corinthians 1:20b–25*).

Parables are not designed to instruct us so much as they are designed to confuse us, to create a stumbling block so that our accustomed ideas are challenged and we can understand in a new way. If the cross is to make sense, we must let go of the way we usually understand. Parables force us to do exactly that. The cross is the stone rejected by many that became the cornerstone of our faith. Without it, there is no faith and, ultimately, no hope. "I have told you this," said Jesus, "so that when [the] hour comes you may re-member that I told you" (*John 16:4*).

Jesus is the parable of God, the unexpected one, the one who invites us to rethink everything: our values, our desires, our self-understanding, and the God in whom we believe. We can stumble over the teaching of Jesus, stumble over the cross. If we remember, however, the words of Jesus, the cross will not be a scandal to us but will be our hope, our refuge, our salvation. The one who comes like a thief in the night will find us waiting.

Conversation

1. *On what basis do people reject the Gospel message? Is it lack of understanding of religious language or resistance to Christian ethic?*

2. *The cross is not about punishment but about love. Do we sometimes twist the meaning of the cross, seeing it as an instrument of God's punishment? How can we let go of the idea of a God who requires suffering?*

3. *What does Paul mean by "the foolishness of God"?*

4. *In what sense is the cross an offense (a scandal)?*

5. *Does reflection on the suffering of Jesus give you courage? Why or why not?*

Silent Reflection/Journal Comments

If I want to see God, I must look at Jesus. If I want to see Jesus, I must look around me. Where in my history and at this time in my life can I see and hear what God is revealing to me?

Invitation to Conversion

Plan a family party, reunion, or celebration that you might not otherwise have decided to do. Celebrate someone in your family or your parish or group who might not otherwise be honored. Surprise someone with your love and generosity.

Closing Prayer

Leader: Let us proclaim the greatness of the Lord;
               Let us rejoice in God our savior.

All: His mercy is from age to age
           to those who fear him.
     He has shown might with his arm,
           dispersed the arrogant of mind and heart.

He has thrown down the rulers from their
        thrones
    but lifted up the lowly.

Leader: The hungry he has filled with good things;
        the rich he has sent away empty.
    He has helped Israel his servant,
        remembering his mercy,

All: according to his promise to our fathers,
        to Abraham and his descendants
        forever.

—Luke 1:50–55

Leader: Glory to the Father and to the Son and to the Holy Spirit

All: as it was in the beginning, is now, and will be forever.
Amen.

Social Time

Resources for Prayer in This Session

Proulx, Richard, and the Cathedral Singers. *Ars Antiqua Choralis Vol. IV: This Is the Day* (CD or cassette). GIA Publications, Inc.

Soper, Scott. *On That Day* (CD or cassette). GIA Publications, Inc.

Resources for Continued Growth

McCracken, David. *The Scandal of the Gospels*: *Jesus, Story, and Offense*. New York: Oxford University Press, 1994.

Praeder, Susan M. *The Word in Women's Worlds*: *Four Parables*. Wilmington, Del.: Michael Glazier, 1988.

The Scandal of the Parables

Bibliography

Bibliography and Other Resources

Alison, James. *Raising Abel: The Recovery of the Eschatological Imagination*. New York: Crossroad Publishing Company, 1966.

Brown, Raymond E., Joseph A. Fitzmyer, and Roland E. Murphy, eds. *The New Jerome Biblical Commentary*. Englewood Cliffs, N.J.: Prentice-Hall Publishing Company, 1990.

Crossan, John Dominic. *The Dark Interval: Toward a Theology of Story*. Sonoma, Calif.: Polebridge Press, 1988.

———. *In Parables*. New York: Harper and Row Publishers, 1973.

Keating, Thomas. *The Kingdom of God Is Like*. New York: Crossroad Publishing Company, 1993.

McCracken, David. *The Scandal of the Gospels: Jesus, Story, and Offense*. New York: Oxford University Press, 1994.

Reid, Barbara. *Parables for Preachers: The Gospel of Luke, Year C*. Collegeville, Minn.: The Liturgical Press, 2000.

Tilley, Terence W. *Story Theology*. Wilmington, Del.: Michael Glazier, 1985.

References to the Catechism of the Catholic Church

Part One, Section One, Chapter Two, Article 3

Part One, Section Two, Chapter Two, Article 3, Paragraph 3

Publishers of Audiovisual Resources

GIA Publications, Inc.
7404 S. Mason Ave.
Chicago, IL 60638-9927
1-800-442-1358
http://www.giamusic.com

St. Anthony Messenger Press
1615 Republic St.
Cincinnati, OH 45210-9989
1-800-488-0488
http://catalog.americancatholic.org

The Publisher

All instructional materials identified by the TAP® (Teachers/Authors/Publishers) trademark are developed by a national network of 460 teacher-authors, whose collective educational experience distinguishes the publishing objective of The Center for Learning, a nonprofit educational corporation founded in 1970.

Concentrating on values-related disciplines, the Center publishes humanities and religion curriculum units for use in public and private schools and other educational settings. Approximately 600 language arts, social studies, novel/drama, life issues, and faith publications are available.

Publications are regularly evaluated and updated to meet the changing and diverse needs of teachers and students. Teachers may offer suggestions for development of new publications or revisions of existing titles by contacting

The Center for Learning
Administration/Creative Development
P.O. Box 417, Evergreen Road
Villa Maria, PA 16155
(800) 767-9090 • FAX (724) 964-1802

The Center for Learning
Editorial/Prepress
24600 Detroit Road, Suite 201
Westlake, OH 44145
(440) 250-9341 • FAX (440) 250-9715

For a free catalog containing order and price
information and a descriptive listing of titles, contact

The Center for Learning
Customer Service
P.O. Box 910, Evergreen Road
Villa Maria, PA 16155
(724) 964-8083 • (800) 767-9090
FAX (888) 767-8080
http://www.centerforlearning.org

Made in the USA
Monee, IL
22 June 2026

55539402R10035